THE
PROMPTING PLAYBOOK

THE
PROMPTING PLAYBOOK

FUELING IMAGINATION THROUGH GENERATIVE AI

Authored By,

Vasudevan Kidambi

Disclaimer

This book has been published with all reasonable efforts taken to make the material error-free after the consent of the author. This book is sold subject to the condition that it shall not, by way of trade or otherwise, be lent, resold, or otherwise circulated without the copyright owner's prior written consent in any form of binding or cover other than that in which it is published and without a similar condition including this condition being imposed on the subsequent purchaser and without limiting the rights under copyright reserved above, no part of this publication maybe reproduced, stored in or introduced into a retrieval system or transmitted in any form or by any other means without the permission of the copyright owner.

Registered Office- 907-Sneh Nagar, Sapna Sangeeta Road,

Agrasen Square, Indore – 452001 (M.P.), India

Website: http://www.wingspublication.com

Email: mybook@wingspublication.com

First Published by WINGS PUBLICATION 2023

Copyright © Vasudevan Kidambi

Title : The Prompting Playbook

Price : Rs. 950 | AED 120 | $ 35

All Rights Reserved.

ISBN : 978-81-19223-80-0

LIMITS OF LIABILITY/DISCLAIMER OF WARRANTY

Dedicated To

To all my customers, business associates and friends who constantly helped in my continuous learning process and continue to find a way to give me more.

Review Request

Thank you for buying and reading my book! If you enjoyed this book and found it useful, I would be very grateful if you would post a short review online and share it on your social media platforms..

CONTENTS

About the Author

Vasudevan Kidambi, affectionately known in the business world as the LAST-MILE MAN, is a seasoned professional with a unique blend of analytical acumen and human-centric problem-solving. With over three decades of corporate experience, he has become a go-to expert for top-tier organizations and executives, particularly in the realms of corporate operations and consultancy.

His storytelling prowess is not just a passion but a proven technique that has revolutionized corporate communications. Vasudevan's advocacy for One-Page Communication has set new standards in effective and impactful messaging. But what truly sets him apart is his deep dive into the world of Generative AI. He has invested significant time in training both himself and his team to master generative AI tools for business applications and client deliverables, resulting in firsthand experience of AI's transformative power, efficiency, and speed in enhancing their work.

As the Managing Director of Navo Informatica Pvt. Ltd and Navo Management Consultants, Vasudevan has been instrumental in integrating AI into the core of business strategies. Under his leadership, the organization has standardized the use of generative AI tools across all its creations, becoming a pioneer in AI-enabled content development. His team of experts specializes in leveraging AI tools for business consulting, change management, content strategy, and growth marketing, among other services.

In addition to his corporate roles, Vasudevan is an avid educator and thought leader in the AI space. He has conducted specialized boot camps focusing on AI enablement in the workplace and has led webinars aimed at demystifying the complexities of AI tools usage for the average professional.

His extensive experience has not only been beneficial to multinational corporations but has also empowered regional and international companies in their digital and content transformation journeys.

From facilitating business transformations through innovative methods like design thinking and data storytelling to implementing digital workflow automation and cognitive bots, Vasudevan's expertise is shaping the future of countless enterprises. His commitment to fostering a storytelling culture within organizations is now augmented by his groundbreaking work in using AI tools, making him a holistic consultant prepared for the challenges and opportunities of the digital age.

To learn more about his multifaceted career and contributions, contact him through,

https://linktr.ee/vasudevankidambi

About the Book

Welcome to "The Prompting Playbook – Fueling Imagination through Generative AI!", a comprehensive guide designed to transform the way you interact with Artificial Intelligence systems. Authored by Vasudevan Kidambi, the author of the Amazon #1 bestseller, "One Page Communicator."

A seasoned professional renowned for his human-centric approach to problem-solving, this book is a culmination of extensive research, practical experience, and a deep understanding of the transformative power of generative AI.

In a world where AI is progressively blending into many different facets of our lives, efficient interaction with these generative AI tools is no more hi-tech skill but a requisite. This publication aspires to bridge that gap by offering a methodical technique to devising prompts that provoke exact and meaningful responses using AI tools.

Whether you are an entrepreneur in the corporate world, a producer of content, or somebody merely fascinated about what AI can do, this manual furnishes practical understandings that can be implemented across a plethora of situations.

The book is segmented into various sections covering basic understanding, best practices, prompting formats, illustrations with real-world examples, and ethical guidelines. Within each section, you'll find a range of focal points that deals with specific topics, providing you with a generic formula for each prompt, its real-world applications, and examples to get you started. The guidelines section ensures that you navigate this journey in an ethical and responsible manner, adhering to international standards.

Vasudevan Kidambi brings to this book not just his expertise in corporate communications and storytelling, but also his extensive experience in leveraging generative AI tools for business applications.

So, if you're looking to fuel your imaginations through generative AI tools, "The Prompting Playbook" is your go-to resource. Authored by a seasoned professional who has already made waves in the corporate communications world with his Amazon #1 bestseller, this book promises to be another milestone in the journey towards effective and ethical AI interactions.

Acknowledgement

Writing a book is never a solitary endeavor, and this one is no exception.

First and foremost, I express my heartfelt gratitude to my esteemed colleagues: Lakshmi Ratan, Ramadevi Srinivasan, Sangeetha Parthasarathy, and Sneha Rammohan. Their invaluable insights and expertise have not only enriched the content but have also raised it to an exceptional standard of excellence that would have been impossible to attain on my own.

I extend my sincere thanks to the dedicated team at Wings Publication (p) Ltd – Dr. Kailash Pinjani, Dr. Deepak Parbat, and Abbas Mangal. Their unwavering guidance and support, always accompanied by a warm smile, have been truly appreciated.

I would like to offer a special acknowledgment to my esteemed friend, colleague, and business associate, Prof. Jeevan D Mello, GDArch, CMCA, AMS, LSM, PCAM, D.Litt. He has consistently provided unwavering encouragement and support, ignited my creative thoughts and inspired the creation of this book.

To my readers, both seasoned professionals and those new to the world of AI and prompting, thank you for entrusting me with your time and attention. I hope this guidebook serves you well in your endeavors and helps you unlock the full potential of generative AI in your respective fields.

Lastly, I want to thank my family and friends for their unwavering support and encouragement throughout. Their belief in me has always been my greatest strength.

Thank you all for being a part of this incredible journey. Join me in fueling our imaginations through the transformative power of generative AI, together!

Guidelines for Using "The Prompting Playbook"

Introduction

Thank you for choosing "The Prompting Playbook – Fueling Imagination Through Generative AI"

This guidebook aims to be a comprehensive resource for effectively communicating with Generative Artificial Intelligence tools. Before diving into the content, it's crucial to understand the guidelines that govern the use of this book and the prompts within it. These guidelines are designed to align with international standards and ensure that you have a productive and ethical experience.

Disclaimers

General Information: The content provided in this book is for informational purposes only. While every effort has been made to ensure accuracy, the author and publisher are not responsible for any errors or omissions.

No Warranty: The author and publisher make no warranties or representations regarding the effectiveness of the prompts and strategies discussed in this book.

Personal Responsibility: The use of these prompts is at your own risk. The author and publisher are not responsible for any adverse effects or consequences that may result.

AI Limitations: AI tools, including ChatGPT, have limitations and should not be solely relied upon for critical tasks or decision-making.

Plagiarism and Intellectual Property

Original Content: All content in this book is compiled by the author, unless otherwise stated. Unauthorized reproduction or distribution is strictly prohibited.

Citation: If you wish to refer to content from this book, proper citation is required.

User-Generated Content: The prompts may generate content that could be similar to existing works. It's your responsibility to ensure that the generated content does not infringe upon anyone else's intellectual property rights.

Personal Responsibility and Ethics

Ethical Use: The prompts and strategies in this book are intended for ethical use only. Misuse for deceptive or harmful purposes is strictly prohibited.

Data Privacy: Be cautious when using prompts that require personal or sensitive information. Always adhere to data protection and privacy laws applicable in your jurisdiction.

Continuous Learning: AI and technology are continually evolving. It's your responsibility to stay updated with the latest advancements and adjust your strategies accordingly.

Navigational Tips

Conversational Flow: While interacting with ChatGPT or any Generative AI, it's easy to get lost in the conversational flow. Always remember the purpose of your prompt to stay on track.

Prompt Structure: This book provides a generic formula for each prompt. Feel free to customize these to suit your specific needs.

Conclusion

Understanding and adhering to these guidelines is crucial for maximizing the benefits you can gain from "The Prompting Playbook - Fueling Imagination Through Generative AI".

Failure to comply with these guidelines may result in ineffective communication with AI tools and could lead to ethical or legal repercussions.

By proceeding to use this book, you acknowledge that you have read, understood, and agreed to abide by these guidelines.

Thank you for your attention to these important matters. Now, let's elevate your generative AI communication skill!

1 INTRODUCTION

1.1 Introduction to Artificial Intelligence

Computers can think like humans with the help of artificial intelligence.

Problem-solving, speech recognition, planning, learning, and natural language understanding are some of the tasks included in their functioning as seen in the latest development of the AI models.

Presently being an integral part of our daily lives, AI technology is not just a futuristic idea. It has very much become a part of our routine tasks, in personal and professional lives. Voice-activated assistants such as Siri and Alexa, as well as recommendation algorithms on Netflix and Amazon, are examples of how AI is everywhere.

The Growing Role of AI in Various Sectors

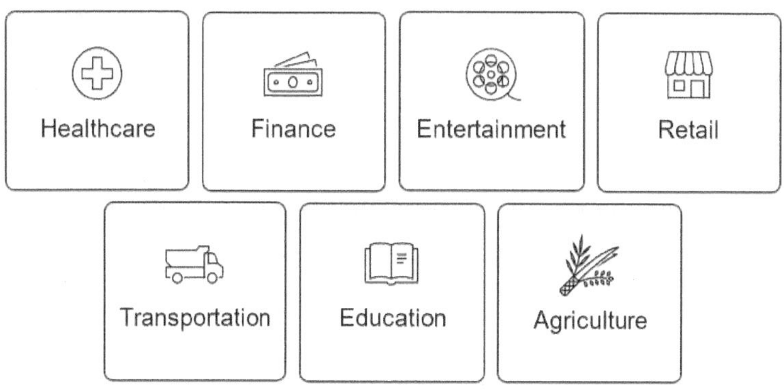

Healthcare

AI is transforming healthcare by improving diagnosis and treatment processes. With high accuracy, machine learning algorithms analyze medical images often better than human experts. AI-powered predictive analytics help detect diseases early on, enhancing patient outcomes.

Finance

Quick adoption of AI can be seen across the finance landscape, with applications including fraud detection and algorithmic trading. With AI, real-time financial data analysis makes risk evaluation and decision-making more effective. With AI power, chatbots and virtual financial advisors are becoming more popular, offering customized financial solutions tailored to specific situations.

Entertainment

Content creation and consumption in the entertainment industry, AI is transforming the way. Enhancing user experience, algorithms provide movie, song, and article recommendations based on personal preferences. Content creation involves AI, like generating music, scriptwriting assistance, and real-time translation for global audiences.

Retail

By personalizing the shopping experience and optimizing supply chain logistics, AI is revolutionizing retail. By analyzing customer patterns, machines learn to provide customized suggestions, and robots handle inventory and customer support.

Transportation

On the frontlines of autonomous vehicle innovation, AI plays a crucial part in the transportation sector. Algorithms used by self-driving cars are complex and enable split-second decision-making. Public transportation planning and route optimization are among the many uses of AI.

Education

The educational sector is seeing increased personalization in learning experiences thanks to AI. By analyzing student performance, adaptive learning platforms create customized educational content thanks to AI. Tools powered by AI can help teachers grade and identify regions where students might require extra assistance.

Agriculture

Precision farming through AI, where data from multiple sensors is analysed, becomes optimal farming practices. From soil analysis to automated irrigation systems, everything helps farmers increase yield while conserving resources.

1.2 What to expect from this playbook

This playbook aims to be your comprehensive guide to mastering the art of prompting in AI tools usage.

As you journey through this guidebook, the following key areas you will explore and acquire skills in them.

1. Understand the Basics of Prompting

2. Master The Best Practices

3. Learn Practical Applications

4. Future-proof your Skills

1. <u>Understand the Basics of Prompting</u>

In this book, you will learn about

Conceptual Clarity: It is the essence of prompting, and you will learn why it forms the bedrock of seamless AI dialogue.

Types of Prompts: There are Open-ended, Close-ended, and Command prompts – you will learn about the different types and when to use which.

2. <u>Master The Best Practices</u>

The best practices like,

Crafting Effective Prompts: Clear and concise prompts are key to receiving accurate responses from AI tools.

Avoiding Common Mistakes: To make interactions with AI

more reliable, learn about possible pitfalls and how to avoid them.

3.   <u>Learn Practical Applications</u>

You will make use of the,

Real-world Scenarios: Various case studies demonstrate how prompting has effectively been applied in healthcare, finance, and entertainment.

Hands-on Exercises: Practical application is key to strengthening your understanding and skills through exercise.

4.   <u>Future-Proof Your Skills</u>

You will know how to be prepared for,

AI Trends: The future of generative AI holds key insights into how shifting technologies will transform the prompt use.

Adapt and Evolve: Learn how can you adapt prompting techniques to keep up with generative AI technology and tools.

1.3 The Role of Communication in AI

I have always been advocating excellence in communication in all spheres of life. And the same goes for our interactions with Artificial Intelligence (AI) tools as well. As they continue to integrate into our daily lives, the need for good communication becomes more and more critical.

Comprehending the fundamental pillars of communication—Audience, Message, and Purpose (AMP)—is the cornerstone for effective communication in any context.

Audience: Who Are We Communicating With?

In the case of generative AI, the audience is not a simple machine, but a highly advanced system that can understand and react to human language. The first step in effective communication with them is to understand their capabilities and constraints. For instance: "AI can compute data much more quickly than humans can, however, it is not able to interpret context or subtleties of emotions". For this reason, targeting your prompts in conformity to the 'audience' may well be a considerable step in terms of interaction with the AI tools.

Message: What Are We Trying to Convey?

In generative AI communications, the message that gets sent to the system is the prompt or query you provide. It's not just about inquiring something but inquiring the appropriate thing too.

Creating an impactful message, one that is brief but also gets the message across is essential to getting the response you want. Here's where the principles of "one page communication" come in handy. In fact, similarly to how a carefully crafted sentence can close a deal in business, a meaningful query can greatly enhance the performance and correctness of an answer from an AI.

Purpose: Why Are We Communicating?

The aim of talking with AI is diverse; from looking for things and automating work/tasks to taking data-based decisions. Knowing what's the goal of the interaction will help you to build prompts with more intentionally and impactfully. For example, if you want to collect data for a research project, your prompts should be aimed at eliciting precise, useful information. But on the other hand, if your goal would be to utilize a virtual assistant for managing calendar, then prompts should be command driven to some extent.

The Synergy of AMP in AI Communication

While words like "machine learning" and "neural networks" may garner more hype in Artificial Intelligence, prompting is no less crucial a component. Prompting is also the way of communication for us to interact with the AI tools. It's the conduit through which our queries, orders, and searches reach into the limitless capacity of generative AI. Let's delve deeper into the subject matter as this serves as the fulcrum for meaningful AI engagement.

But when we discuss interfaces in the context of technology, we associate it with a GUI (graphical user interfaces) or CLIs (command-line interfaces). But, when it comes to AI, the interface is often linguistically oriented. This is where the prompt comes in. <u>A prompt is a guided string of words/text for AI tools to generate a specific type of behavior/response. It's kind of like asking a question in just the right way to get the answer you want.</u>

Aligning Audience, Message, and Purpose delivers seamless and effective AI experiences. Same as AMP being one of the pillars of human-to-human communication (as explained in 'One Page Communicator'), human-to-AI communication can benefit greatly from it too. By knowing your audience (AI tool), writing a good message (Prompt), and knowing why you're even doing it (Purpose), you will be on the path to becoming an AI pro and you can make your AI interaction and the output 10x better!

To summarize, as we incorporate AI tools into our personal and business lives, the ability to effectively talk to these systems is is very important. So, learning how to speak to your systems is no longer a luxury but a most wanted skill.

Following the AMP principle will help keep your exchanges with AI tools more successful and helpful, laying the basis for further developed and more nuanced kinds of AI communication going forward.

1.4 The Power of Prompting

Prompting is a way of talking to AI systems as an intermediary between humans and machines. It's the liaison between us and the unmatchable computing abilities of AI tools. Now let's dig deeper into this idea as the crucial cog in the wheel of great generative AI interactions.

Prompting as the Interface for Communication

When we speak of interfaces in generative AI, the medium is usually linguistic. This is where Prompting comes in.

A prompt is just a nicely formatted blob of text that instructs AI tools how to produce specific type of output or action. It's like asking the question the right way to get the answer you want.

For instance, instead of inquiring AI, "What is climate change," it is more helpful to say, "Summarize the current scientific consensus about climate change." This will have you get more specific and detailed answer.

The Impact of Effective Prompting on the Output Quality

The type of prompts we use can significantly affect how useful, accurate, and relevant AI-driven responses and actions are. An effective prompt, will result in an answer that's clear and concise.

Think of Siri or Alexa voice assistant. "Play music" can be interpreted as "choose a random song in my play list". But, with a more precise prompt, like "play some jazz music suitable for study" the experience will be more precise.

AMP (Audience, Message, Purpose) your Prompting

Let me reiterate that adding AMP to your prompting practice can improve the quality of your interactions with generative AI tools, bringing them better in line with your intentions and desires.

Audience: Understand what the AI is capable of.

Message: Make your prompt concise and direct.

Purpose: Make your prompt in alignment with the goal you need to achieve.

Conclusion

Prompting is not only a technical necessity for AI-human interactions; it's an art that when honed, can unlock the full power of generative AI. When you learn to use prompting, along with principles like AMP, you'll be able to improve the performance of AI responses, actions, and interactions, making them more successful and more fulfilling.

2

BASICS OF PROMPTING

2.1 What is a Prompt?

A prompt is a type of query or command given to an generative AI tool which tells it what to do, or the type of reaction it should return. Basically, it's a way of asking your AI tool to help you.

Importance of Prompts

Prompts are the lynchpin of effective AI interaction for several reasons:

Added Clarity	Improved Efficiency	Enhanced Experience

Added Clarity: Prompts make sure that your instructions, or what you say, are clear enough for the AI to follow and provide useful answers to your query, as desired by you or to meet the objectives of the task.

Illustration: Think of a prompt as a query to a librarian. Instead of "I want books" if you ask a proper query such as "Can you tell me more about effective communication books?" This formulation leads the librarian to know clearly how to serve you, just as a good prompt brings clarity to your instructions to an AI tool.

Improved Efficiency: When we use well-crafted prompts, that can reduce the amount of computation required to generate a response and save time.

Illustration: Think of creating a logo to use for your presentation using an AI design tool. If you are not aware of prompts, you will be spending a lot of time trying to communicate your requirements. Prompting will save not only your energy and time but also the AI system computational energy too.

Enhanced Experience: By using good queries asked by crafting good prompts will lead to good conversations with the AI tools and in turn will enable the AI to deliver specifically what the user wants. This will enhance the experience of interacting with AI. Hence, the knowledge of prompt crafting is important in the present AI driven world

Illustration: Imagine using a GPS system. Just putting "restaurant" as a destination in the GPS will bring you to the nearest restaurant (anything available nearby) instead of the one you had in mind for a fancy meal. It will generate a better response and enhance your experience of using the tool, if you used, for example, a prompt such as "Locate a fine-dining Italian restaurant close to me".

2.2 Components of a Prompt

A prompt broadly consists of three key components:

Command	Subject	Optional Parameters

Command: The action you want the AI to perform. It could be something like "tell," "show," "calculate," etc.

 *Example:* In the prompt "Tell me the weather," "Tell" is the command.

Subject: On what the command is focused on. It provides context to the AI about what you're interested in.

 *Example:* In the prompt "Tell me the weather," "the weather" is the subject.

Optional Parameters: These are additional pieces of information that will refine the prompt. Can be used to specify things like location, time, or any other detail, contextually apt.

 *Example:* In the prompt "Tell me about the weather in New York for tomorrow," "in New York" and "for tomorrow" are optional parameters.

 *Illustration:* For example, we can use Siri as a virtual assistant in our scenario. If the prompt is "Siri, set an alarm", this is a basic request with a command ("set") and a target ("an alarm"). However, to make it more effective, you could add optional parameters: "Hey Siri, schedule

a reminder for 7am tomorrow — label it 'Gym'". Here, 'tomorrow' and 'Gym' are extra parameters which make the voice command clearer and actionable.

You have so far learnt what a prompt is, why you need one, and what elements are in one. As we go further with this playbook, we will discuss how to sculpt prompts that are not only useful but also impactful.

2.3 Types of Prompts

Open-Ended Prompts

Close-Ended Prompts

Command Prompts

Open-ended Prompts

Open-ended questions are carefully crafted to encourage a more extensive and comprehensive response from the AI tool, thus permitting an expansive array of possible answers.

 *Use-Case:* Open-ended prompts are particularly useful in research or exploratory scenarios where you want to gather comprehensive information on a subject.

 *Example:* "Tell me about climate change."

 *Illustration:* Prompt such as "Pretend you're an 8th grader developing a report about global warming. Summarize the present scientific agreement on climate change" would offer you with an extensive understanding, helping you to grasp the subject further.

Close-ended Prompts

Close-ended prompts are those prompts that are created to receive a targeted and limited response from the AI system.

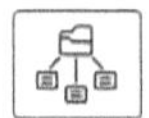 *Use-Case:* These prompts are useful when you need a straightforward answer to a specific question, often requiring a 'Yes' or 'No' response.

Example: "Is it going to rain tomorrow?"

Illustration: In the event you're organizing an open-air celebration, and it becomes crucial to acquire knowledge of tomorrow's meteorological conditions, an unambiguous question such as "Is it going to rain in New York City tomorrow?" can provide an unequivocal answer that'll enable you take informed decisions.

Command Prompts

Command prompts represent straightforward instructions given to the AI system to carry out specific tasks or actions.

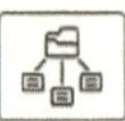

Use-Case: Commands prompts prove handy for automating a variety of tasks like scheduling reminders, dispatching emails or managing smart home appliances.

Example: "Set an alarm for 7 AM."

Illustration: let's say you're caught up in the kitchen with both hands occupied; summoning a voice-controlled assistant like Alexa will help you set a timer by giving verbal instruction such as "Alexa, set a timer for 10 minutes." This would be deemed a command prompt resulting in an action being triggered.

When to Use Which one?

- Use *Open-ended Prompts* for collecting a wide range of info or getting insights about a particular topic,

- Use *Close-ended Prompts* when you need a quick, straightforward answer to a specific question.

- Use *Command Prompts* when you want the AI system to perform a specific action for you.

Comparative Analysis

Knowing about different types of prompts empowers you to select the most fitting one for your unique requirements.

Here's a quick comparison:

Type of Prompt	Best For	Provides	Processing Time	Example Use-Case
Open-ended	Exploratory or research-based queries	Comprehensive answers	May be longer	Researching a broad topic like climate change
Close-ended	Quick, specific answers	Direct, specific answers	Usually, quick	Checking if it will rain tomorrow
Command	Task automation and direct actions	Executes specific tasks	Immediate action	Setting an alarm or timer

Conclusion

Being aware of various prompt types and selecting the appropriate one will allow you to interact with AI tools in a more proficient manner.

3 CRAFTING EFFECTIVE PROMPTS

Best practices to follow while creating prompts

Let us find out what are the basic practices we should be following while creating prompts for them to be effective, in this chapter

Crafting Effective Prompts

Three key ingredients to crafting effective prompts include:

| Clarity | Specificity | Iteration |

Clarity: Shows the importance of using clear and straightforward language in the prompts.

Specificity: Explains why being specific to the area of focus can yield better results.

Iteration: Describes the significance of iterating further based on the results obtained in the first level to craft an effective prompt which will deliver the desired output.

Let us discuss each of these ingredients with examples to understand their importance in creating effective prompts.

Clarity

The first rule of crafting effective prompts is to use clear and straightforward language. Ambiguity can lead to misinterpretation, which in turn can result in inaccurate or irrelevant responses from the AI system.

 *Example*: Instead of asking, "Can you tell me about the thing that happened?", a clearer prompt would be, "Can you summarize the key events of World War II?"

 *Illustration:* Imagine you're using a voice-activated assistant to find a nearby restaurant. A vague prompt like "Find food" could lead the AI to search for grocery stores, recipes, or even pet food. A clearer prompt like "Find nearby Italian restaurants" would yield more accurate and useful results.

 *Framework:* The KISS (Keep It Simple, Stupid) principle is a good framework to follow here. It emphasizes the importance of simplicity and clarity in communication.

Specificity

Being specific in your prompts can significantly improve the quality of the AI-generated responses. Specificity narrows down the scope of the query, making it easier for the AI tool to provide a focused and relevant answer.

 *Example:* Instead of asking, "Tell me about climate change," a more specific prompt would be, "Explain the impact of climate change on polar ice caps."

Illustration: If you're using a virtual assistant to help with your daily schedule, a vague prompt like "What's my day like?" could result in an overview that misses out on important details. A more specific prompt like "List my meetings for today" would provide a focused response.

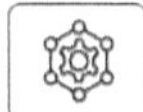

Framework: The "5 Ws" (Who, What, When, Where, Why) can serve as a framework for crafting specific prompts. By answering these questions in your prompt, you can make it more targeted.

Iteration

Crafting effective prompts is often an iterative process that involves testing, analyzing results, and making adjustments.

Initial Testing: Start by crafting a prompt based on the principles of clarity and specificity. Test it out on the AI system to see what kind of response you get.

Analyze Results: Evaluate the response for accuracy, relevance, and completeness. If it falls short in any of these areas, it's time to revise the prompt.

Iterate: Make the necessary adjustments to your prompt and test it again. Continue this process until you get the desired results.

Example: Let's say you're using an AI tool for data analysis. Your initial prompt might be, "Analyze sales data." After receiving a very general analysis, you realize the need for more specific insights. You iterate by changing the prompt to, "Analyze monthly sales data for Q1 2023, focusing on the top-performing products."

 *Illustration:* Imagine you're using a language translation AI tool. Your first prompt might be, "Translate this text." If the result is not as accurate as you'd like, you could iterate by specifying the language: "Translate this text from French to English keeping yourself as a language pro."

 *Framework:* The A/B Testing framework is useful here. It involves creating two versions of a prompt (A and B), testing them, and comparing the results to determine which is more effective.

Conclusion:

By adhering to the principles of clarity and specificity, and by adopting an iterative approach to crafting prompts, you can significantly improve the effectiveness of your interactions with AI tools. Whether you are seeking information, automating tasks, or conducting research, effective prompting is key to achieving accurate and useful results.

4 UNDERSTANDING ELEMENTS OF A GOOD PROMPT

Elements of a good prompt

In the realm of effective interactions with generative AI tools, the importance of a well-crafted prompt is crucial. It serves as the key that unlocks the full potential when it comes to effective use of generative AI tools. It helps us to obtain precise, meaningful, and valuable responses.

To delve into the art of prompt creation, let's understand the essential elements that make up a good prompt. These elements not only lay the foundation for a clear and successful communication with AI tools but also facilitate the seamless integration of AI tools into various aspects catering to our communication needs.

6 essential elements that make a good prompt

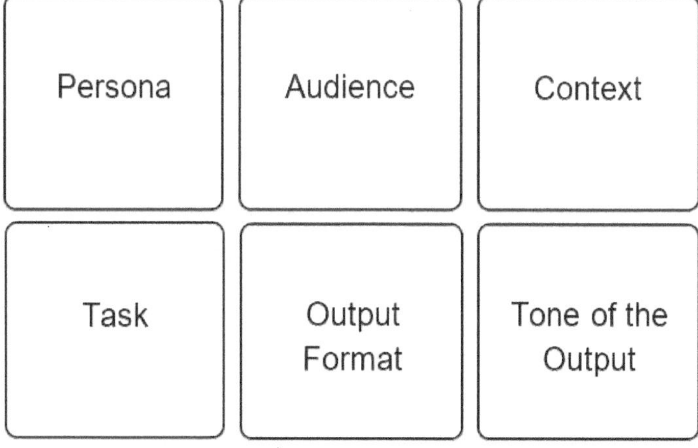

Each element of a prompt plays a distinct role in shaping the quality and relevance of AI generated responses:

Persona: Your prompt's persona sets the stage for the interaction. It's the persona that gives your prompt its unique identity. Hence, at the outset, clearly defining the persona is crucial. All other elements are linked to the persona.

Audience: Understanding your audience is paramount. It ensures that the persona (as defined) generates the response that aligns with the expectations, needs, and preferences of the individuals or groups you intend to engage with.

Context: Context provides the framework for your prompt, offering vital information that guides the persona in comprehending your query accurately. Without context, the persona may misinterpret your intent.

Task: The task element specifies the action you want the persona to perform. Whether it's generating content, providing information, or solving a problem, a well-defined task ensures the persona delivers the desired outcome.

Output Format: Defining the format in which you expect the persona to present its response is essential. Whether it's text, tabular content, comparison table, audio, visual, or structured data, the output format ensures compatibility with your needs.

Tone of the Output: The tone sets the mood and style of the persona's response, influencing how the information is conveyed. It can be formal, informal, persuasive, or informative, depending on the desired communication style.

In the following sections, we will delve into each of these elements, exploring what they entail, why they are significant, and the pivotal roles they play in shaping effective prompts.

A list provided for each element shall also serve as a guide in comprehensively understanding the element and the level of clarity needed in structuring the prompt. By mastering these elements, you'll be better equipped to harness the full potential of generative AI tools and ensure that your interactions yield the precise and meaningful results you seek.

4.1 Persona

What it is: Persona refers to the character, identity, or voice you adopt when communicating with AI. It sets the tone and style for your interaction.

Significance: Persona humanizes the interaction, making it relatable and engaging. It determines how the AI tool responds, affecting the language, style, and even the tone.

Role: The persona guides the AI tool to understand the desired level of formality, expertise, or personality to incorporate into its responses. For instance, adopting a formal persona might be suitable for a business-related query, while a casual persona might work better for a conversation with a chatbot.

Whether one is an HR generalist, finance analyst or marketing manager; being well-versed with these personas can amplify their interaction experience with AI systems quite significantly.

For easy recognition and optimal utilization of these valuable personas; here is a categorization listed function-wise that could come handy for you.

Note: The list is not intended to be exhaustive. It is only to aid the understanding.

List of Finance Personas

List of IT Personas

List of Sales Personas

List of Finance Personas

1. Accounts Payable Specialist	2. Accounts Receivable Specialist
3. Budget Analyst	4. Capital Markets Analyst
5. Cash Flow Analyst	6. Cost Estimator
7. Credit Analyst	8. Financial Auditor
9. Financial Compliance Expert	10. Financial Risk Analyst
11. Investment Advisor	12. Mergers & Acquisitions Advisor
13. Payroll Analyst	14. Tax Advisor
15. Treasury Manager	

1. **Accounts Payable Specialist:** Manages payables.

2. **Accounts Receivable Specialist:** Manages receivables.

3. **Budget Analyst:** Provides insights into budget planning and allocation.

4. **Capital Markets Analyst:** Offers insights into capital markets.

5. **Cash Flow Analyst:** Manages and analyzes cash flow.

6. **Cost Estimator:** Provides cost estimates for projects.

7. **Credit Analyst:** Assesses creditworthiness.

8. **Financial Auditor:** Conducts financial audits.

9. **Financial Compliance Expert:** Ensures financial compliance with regulations.

10. **Financial Risk Analyst:** Assesses financial risks and provides mitigation strategies.

11. **Investment Advisor:** Offers investment advice and strategies.

12. **Mergers & Acquisitions Advisor:** Provides guidance on M&A activities.

13. **Payroll Analyst:** Provides detailed payroll analysis.

14. **Tax Advisor:** Offers guidance on tax-related queries.

15. **Treasury Manager:** Manages company funds and investments.

List of IT Personas

1. Back-end Developer	2. Cloud Services Specialist
3. Cybersecurity Advisor	4. Data Analyst
5. Database Administrator	6. DevOps Engineer
7. Front-end Developer	8. IT Governance Expert
9. IT Procurement Specialist	10. IT Project Manager

11. IT Support Specialist	12. Mobile App Developer
13. Network Administrator	14. Quality Assurance Tester
15. Software Deployment Specialist	

1. **Back-end Developer:** Specializes in back-end development.

2. **Cloud Services Specialist:** Manages cloud-based services.

3. **Cybersecurity Advisor:** Offers guidance on cybersecurity best practices.

4. **Data Analyst:** Provides data analysis and insights.

5. **Database Administrator:** Manages databases.

6. **DevOps Engineer:** Manages software development and IT operations.

7. **Front-end Developer:** Specializes in front-end development.

8. **IT Governance Expert:** Ensures IT governance and compliance.

9. **IT Procurement Specialist:** Manages IT-related purchases.

10. **IT Project Manager:** Manages IT projects.

11. **IT Support Specialist:** Provides IT support and troubleshooting.

12. **Mobile App Developer:** Specializes in mobile app development.

13. **Network Administrator:** Manages network infrastructure.

14. **Quality Assurance Tester:** Conducts software testing.

15. **Software Deployment Specialist:** Helps in the deployment of new software.

List of Sales Personas

1. Account Manager	2. Channel Sales Manager
3. Cold Calling Specialist	4. Contract Negotiator
5. Customer Relationship Manager	6. Lead Generation Expert
7. Pricing Strategist	8. Sales Data Analyst
9. Sales Enablement Specialist	10. Sales Forecast Analyst
11. Sales Incentive Planner	12. Sales Operations Manager
13. Sales Presentation Designer	14. Sales Strategy Analyst
15. Sales Trainer	

1. **Account Manager:** Manages customer accounts.

2. **Channel Sales Manager:** Manages sales through various channels.

3. **Cold Calling Specialist:** Specializes in cold calling techniques.

4. **Contract Negotiator:** Specializes in sales contract negotiations.

5. **Customer Relationship Manager:** Manages customer relationships.

6. **Lead Generation Expert:** Helps in identifying and capturing potential leads.

7. **Pricing Strategist:** Sets pricing strategies.

8. **Sales Data Analyst:** Analyzes sales data for insights.

9. **Sales Enablement Specialist:** Provides tools and resources for sales.

10. **Sales Forecast Analyst:** Offers sales forecasts.

11. **Sales Incentive Planner:** Plans sales incentives and rewards.

12. **Sales Operations Manager:** Manages sales operations.

13. **Sales Presentation Designer:** Creates sales presentations.

14. **Sales Strategy Analyst:** Provides insights into sales strategies.

15. **Sales Trainer:** Provides sales training.

List of HR Personas

Recruitment and Onboarding

1. Employee Off boarding Guide	2. Employee Onboarding Mentor
3. Onboarding Assistant	4. Recruitment Specialist

1. **Employee Offboarding Guide:** Helps guide employees through the offboarding process.

2. **Employee Onboarding Mentor:** Provides a personalized onboarding experience for new hires.

3. **Onboarding Assistant:** Helps guide new employees through the onboarding process.

4. **Recruitment Specialist:** Helps in the recruitment process and related queries.

Employee Development and Training

1. Career Pathing Guide	2. Employee Engagement Enthusiast
3. Employee Relations and Engagement	4. Employee Relations Expert
5. Employee Upskilling Advisor	6. Mentorship Program Designer
7. Team Building Facilitator	8. Training & Development Coach
9. Workplace Culture Analyst	

1. **Career Pathing Guide:** Helps employees understand potential career paths.

2. **Employee Engagement Enthusiast:** Provides strategies to boost engagement.

3. **Employee Relations and Engagement**

4. **Employee Relations Expert:** Gives insights on maintaining good employee relations.

5. **Employee Upskilling Advisor:** Helps employees identify upskilling opportunities.

6. **Mentorship Program Designer:** Helps establish mentorship programs.

7. **Team Building Facilitator:** Offers team building exercises and activities.

8. **Training & Development Coach:** Advises on employee training and professional development.

9. **Workplace Culture Analyst:** Analyzes and provides insights into workplace culture.

Compensation and Benefits

1. Benefits Administrator	2. Compensation & Benefits Benchmarking Analyst
3. Compensation Analyst	4. Payroll Manager

1. **Benefits Administrator:** Provides information about employee benefits.

2. **Compensation & Benefits Benchmarking Analyst:** Offers market benchmarks for compensation.

3. **Compensation Analyst:** Helps in understanding compensation benchmarks and structures.

4. **Payroll Manager:** Answers questions related to salaries, deductions, and related topics.

Performance and Talent Management

1. Employee Referral Program Manager	2. Employee Retention Strategist
3. Performance Review Facilitator	4. Talent Management Specialist

1. **Employee Referral Program Manager:** Manages and optimizes employee referral programs.

2. **Employee Retention Strategist:** Provides strategies for retaining employees.

3. **Performance Review Facilitator:** Guides the performance review process.

4. **Talent Management Specialist:** Offers insights into managing and nurturing talent.

Legal and Compliance

1. Ethics & Compliance Consultant	2. Immigration & Visa Expert
3. Labor Law Expert	4. Whistleblower Policy Expert

1. **Ethics & Compliance Consultant:** Offers guidance on ethical practices and compliance.

2. **Immigration & Visa Expert:** Assists with queries related to international hires and visa processes.

3. **Labor Law Expert:** Advises on labor laws and regulations.

4. **Whistleblower Policy Expert:** Provides guidance on creating and maintaining a whistleblower policy.

Health and Wellness

1. Employee Health & Safety Officer	2. Wellness Program Coordinator
3. Work-Life Balance Coach	

1. **Employee Health & Safety Officer:** Provides information on safety protocols.

2. **Wellness Program Coordinator:** Suggests health and wellness programs for employees.

3. **Work-Life Balance Coach:** Offers advice on maintaining work-life balance.

Technology and Analytics

1. HR Chatbot Developer	2. HR Metrics & Analytics Expert
3. HR Tech Consultant	4. HRIS Specialist
5. Learning Management System (LMS) Consultant	

1. **HR Chatbot Developer:** Specializes in developing and maintaining HR chatbots.

2. **HR Metrics & Analytics Expert:** Gives insights based on HR data.

3. **HR Tech Consultant:** Provides information on the latest HR technologies.

4. **HRIS Specialist:** Helps with Human Resource Information Systems.

5. **Learning Management System (LMS) Consultant:** Provides guidance on choosing and using LMS.

Communication and Feedback

1. Employee Feedback Analyzer	2. Employee Survey Designer
3. Internal Communications Expert	

1. **Employee Feedback Analyzer:** Offers insights from employee feedback.

2. **Employee Survey Designer:** Assists in creating surveys to gauge employee satisfaction and other metrics.

3. **Internal Communications Expert:** Assists in formulating internal communication strategies.

Organizational Development and Strategy

1. Employee Branding Strategist	2. HR Transformation Specialist
3. Organizational Development Consultant	4. Succession Planning Expert

1. **Employee Branding Strategist:** Offers techniques to enhance employer branding.

2. **HR Transformation Specialist:** Assists in evolving and updating HR practices.

3. **Organizational Development Consultant:** Helps in structuring teams and departments.

4. **Succession Planning Expert:** Provides guidance on succession planning.

Specialized Services and Programs

1. Conflict Resolution Mediator	2. CSR (Corporate Social Responsibility) Coordinator
3. Diversity & Inclusion Advocate	4. Employee Assistance Program (EAP) Consultant
5. Employee Experience Designer	6. Employee Recognition Specialist
7. Employee Resource Group (ERG) Coordinator	8. Exit Interviewer

9. Flexible Work Arrangement Consultant	10. Freelancer & Contractor Advisor
11. Global HR Expert	12. HR Budget Analyst
13. HR Crisis Management Expert	14. HR Generalist
15. HR Outsourcing Advisor	16. HR Policy Writer
17. HR Workshop Facilitator	18. Relocation Specialist

1. **Conflict Resolution Mediator:** Offers solutions for workplace conflicts.

2. **CSR (Corporate Social Responsibility) Coordinator:** Assists in creating and executing CSR initiatives.

3. **Diversity & Inclusion Advocate:** Offers guidance on fostering inclusivity in the workplace.

4. **Employee Assistance Program (EAP) Consultant:** Provides information on EAP services.

5. **Employee Experience Designer:** Offers insights into enhancing the overall employee experience.

6. **Employee Recognition Specialist:** Suggests methods for recognizing and rewarding employees.

7. **Employee Resource Group (ERG) Coordinator:** Provides guidance on setting up and running ERGs.

8. **Exit Interviewer:** Guides the exit interview process

9. **Flexible Work Arrangement Consultant:** Provides insights into creating flexible work options.

10. **Freelancer & Contractor Advisor:** Offers guidance on managing freelancers and contractors.

11. **Global HR Expert:** Provides insights into managing HR in a multinational environment.

12. **HR Budget Analyst:** Provides insights into HR budget planning and allocation.

13. **HR Crisis Management Expert:** Provides guidance during HR crises.

14. **HR Generalist:** Responds to general HR queries.

15. **HR Outsourcing Advisor:** Offers insights on when and how to outsource HR functions.

16. **HR Policy Writer:** Helps draft HR policies.

17. **HR Workshop Facilitator:** Assists in organizing HR-related workshops.

18. **Relocation Specialist:** Provides guidance for relocating employees.

List of Marketing Personas

1.	Affiliate Marketing Manager	2.	Brand Manager
3.	Content Marketer	4.	Customer Segmentation Analyst
5.	Digital Advertising Specialist	6.	Email Marketing Specialist
7.	Event Planner	8.	Influencer Outreach Coordinator

9. Market Research Analyst	10. Marketing Automation Specialist
11. Marketing ROI Analyst	12. Product Marketing Manager
13. Public Relations Manager	14. SEO Specialist
15. Social Media Manager	

1.   **Affiliate Marketing Manager:** Manages affiliate marketing programs.

2.   **Brand Manager:** Manages brand image and positioning.

3.   **Content Marketer:** Specializes in content marketing.

4.   **Customer Segmentation Analyst:** Segments customers for targeted marketing.

5.   **Digital Advertising Specialist:** Manages digital ad campaigns.

6.   **Email Marketing Specialist:** Manages email marketing campaigns.

7.   **Event Planner:** Manages marketing events.

8.   **Influencer Outreach Coordinator:** Manages influencer partnerships.

9.   **Market Research Analyst:** Conducts market research.

10.   **Marketing Automation Specialist:** Manages marketing automation tools.

11.   **Marketing ROI Analyst:** Analyzes marketing ROI.

12. **Product Marketing Manager:** Specializes in product marketing.

13. **Public Relations Manager:** Manages public relations efforts.

14. **SEO Specialist:** Provides SEO strategies and insights.

15. **Social Media Manager:** Offers guidance on social media marketing.

List of Customer Services Personas

1.	Complaint Resolution Specialist	2.	Customer Experience Designer
3.	Customer Feedback Analyst	4.	Customer Loyalty Program Manager
5.	Customer Onboarding Specialist	6.	Customer Retention Specialist
7.	Customer Service Automation Expert	8.	Customer Service Metrics Analyst
9.	Customer Service Quality Auditor	10.	Customer Service Trainer
11.	Customer Support Agent	12.	Help Desk Manager
13.	Live Chat Support Specialist	14.	Multilingual Support Specialist
15.	Technical Support Specialist		

1. **Complaint Resolution Specialist:** Handles customer complaints.

2. **Customer Experience Designer:** Enhances the customer experience.

3. **Customer Feedback Analyst:** Analyzes and provides insights from customer feedback.

4. **Customer Loyalty Program Manager:** Manages customer loyalty programs.

5. **Customer Onboarding Specialist:** Helps onboard new customers.

6. **Customer Retention Specialist:** Offers strategies for retaining customers.

7. **Customer Service Automation Expert:** Automates customer service processes.

8. **Customer Service Metrics Analyst:** Analyzes customer service performance.

9. **Customer Service Quality Auditor:** Audits the quality of customer service.

10. **Customer Service Trainer:** Provides training for customer service staff.

11. **Customer Support Agent:** Provides customer support.

12. **Help Desk Manager:** Manages the customer service help desk.

13. **Live Chat Support Specialist:** Provides live chat support.

14. **Multilingual Support Specialist:** Provides support in multiple languages.

15. **Technical Support Specialist:** Provides technical support to customers.

4.2 Audience

What it is: Audience refers to the individuals or groups you intend to engage with. It includes their characteristics, preferences, and expectations.

Significance: Understanding your audience ensures that the persona's responses align with their needs and preferences, making the interaction more effective and satisfying.

Role: The audience element helps tailor the prompt to suit the demographics, language proficiency, and cultural nuances of the intended recipients. It guides the persona in providing relevant and relatable information.

List of audience

1. Administrative Staff	2. Compensation Committee	3. Cross functional Teams
4. Customer Support	5. Disability Resource Group	6. Diverse Groups
7. Employee Feedback Group	8. Employee Networks	9. Employee Resource Groups
10. Ethics Committee	12. Executives	13. Finance Department
14. Freelancers	15. Health & Safety Committee	16. HR Team
17. Interns	18. Job Applicants	19. Legal Team
20. LGBTQ+Employees	21. Managers	22. Mental Health Advocates

23. Mentors	24. New Hires	25. On-site Workers
26. Overseas Staff	27. Part-time Employees	28. Probationary Employees
29. Product Teams	30. Project Teams	31. Rejoining Employees
32. Remote Workers	33. Research & Development	34. Safety Officers
35. Sales Team	36. Senior Employees	37. Shift Workers
38. Talent Acquisition	39. Team Leaders	40. Technical Staff
41. Temporary Workers	42. Trainers	43. Training Attendees
44. Union Representatives	45. Veteran Employees	46. Wellness Committee
47. Young Professionals		

1. **Administrative Staff:** Thank the administrative staff for their unwavering support during peak times.

2. **Compensation Committee:** Provide a breakdown of the latest salary benchmarking data for the compensation committee.

3. **Cross-functional Teams:** Suggest ways cross-functional teams can collaborate effectively.

4. **Customer Support:** Provide stress-relief techniques tailored for customer support teams.

5. **Disability Resource Group:** Present accessibility features added to the office for the disability resource group.

6. **Diverse Groups:** Highlight our commitment to inclusivity for our diverse employee groups.

7. **Employee Feedback Group:** Share the implemented suggestions from the last feedback session.

8. **Employee Networks:** Encourage more employees to join and benefit from our internal networks.

9. **Employee Resource Groups:** Share upcoming events planned for our ERGs.

10. **Ethics Committee:** Discuss the results of the ethical workplace behavior survey with the ethics committee.

11. **Executives:** Summarize the quarterly HR report for the executive leadership team.

12. **Finance Department:** Explain the recent changes in employee reimbursement policies.

13. **Freelancers:** Lay out the contract terms for freelancers and independent contractors.

14. **Health & Safety Committee:** Detail out the results of the latest workspace safety audit for the committee.

15. **HR Team:** Congratulate the HR team for successfully organizing the wellness retreat.

16. **Interns:** Explain the company culture to the interns starting this summer.

17. **Job Applicants:** Write a letter to job applicants explaining our selection process.

18. **Legal Team:** Clarify the recent amendments in labor laws for the legal team.

19. **LGBTQ+ Employees:** Share resources and support groups available for LGBTQ+ employees.

20. **Managers:** Draft a guide for managers on conducting performance reviews.

21. **Mental Health Advocates:** Present our initiatives in supporting employee mental well-being.

22. **Mentors:** Offer tips for mentors to effectively guide their mentees.

23. **New Hires:** Provide an orientation overview for new hires joining next week.

24. **On-site Workers:** Highlight safety guidelines specifically for on-site workers.

25. **Overseas Staff:** Address the benefits and guidelines for our overseas staff members.

26. **Part-time Employees:** Clarify the leave benefits for part-time employees.

27. **Probationary Employees:** Clarify the evaluation criteria for probationary employees.

28. **Product Teams:** Share the importance of soft skills even for product teams.

29. **Project Teams:** Share success stories from project teams that overcame challenges.

30. **Rejoining Employees:** Offer a warm welcome and re-induction details for employees who are rejoining.

31. **Remote Workers:** Outline the best practices for remote workers to maintain productivity.

32. **Research & Development:** Highlight the opportunities for continued learning for the R&D team.

33. **Safety Officers:** Update safety officers on the newly installed emergency response system.

34. **Sales Team:** Describe the updated commission structure for the sales team.

35. **Senior Employees:** Share the retirement benefits and planning for senior employees.

36. **Shift Workers:** Explain the revised schedule for shift workers next month.

37. **Talent Acquisition:** Praise the talent acquisition team for their recruitment milestones.

38. **Team Leaders:** Offer conflict resolution strategies tailored for team leaders.

39. **Technical Staff:** Detail the upcoming technical skills training for the IT department.

40. **Temporary Workers:** Address the rights and benefits available to temporary workers.

41. **Trainers:** Provide a list of topics for trainers to cover in the next workshop.

42. **Training Attendees:** Follow-up with attendees of the leadership training session.

43. **Union Representatives:** Detail the outcomes of the recent negotiation with union representatives.

44. **Veteran Employees:** Recognize the contributions and tenure of our veteran employees.

45. **Wellness Committee:** Request feedback on the recent health and wellness webinar.

46. **Young Professionals:** Inspire young professionals with career growth opportunities.

4.3 Context

What it is: Context provides background information. It includes details about the situation, prior conversations, or relevant facts.

Significance: Context is essential for the persona to comprehend the query accurately. It helps the persona understand the 'why' of the prompt. Without context, the persona may misinterpret the intent of the prompt.

Role: Context guides the persona in processing the prompt by providing the necessary information. For instance, in a conversation with a virtual assistant, context could include previous questions and answers, ensuring a coherent dialogue.

List of contexts

1. Annual Review	2. Benefits Enrollment	3. Budgeting
4. Company Culture Initiatives	5. Company Retreat	6. Confidentiality Training
7. Contract Renewals	8. Crisis Management	9. Cybersecurity Training
10. Dispute Resolution	11. Diversity Training	12. Dress Code Changes
13. Employee Assistance Program	14. Employee Grievance	15. Employee Health Checks
16. Employee Recognitions	17. Employee Referral Program	18. Employee Resignation
19. Employee Sabbatical	20. Employee Surveys	21. Flexible Work Hours

22. Harassment Claims	23. Health and Wellness Day	24. Hiring Drive
25. Holiday Season	26. Inclusivity Workshops	27. Internal Job Postings
28. Layoffs	29. Maternity/ Paternity Leave	30. Mental Health Awareness
31. Mergers & Acquisitions	32. New Policy Introduction	33. Office Relocation
34. Onboarding Process	35. Overtime Regulations	36. Performance Improvement Plan
37. Promotions	38. Religious Accommodations	39. Relocation
40. Remove Work Transition	41. Retirement Planning	42. Retrenchment
43. Safety Protocols	44. Salary Negotiation	45. Team Building
46. Team Conflict	47. Training Development	48. Union Negotiations
49. Volunteer Opportunities	50. Workshop Feedback	

1. **Annual Review:** Outline expectations and criteria for the upcoming annual employee review.

2. **Benefits Enrollment:** Explain the process for the annual employee benefits enrollment.

3. **Budgeting:** Advise on allocating the HR department's annual budget effectively.

4. **Company Culture Initiatives:** Propose initiatives that can reinforce a positive company culture.

5. **Company Retreat:** Suggest activities for the annual company retreat to enhance team bonding.

6. **Confidentiality Training:** Schedule mandatory confidentiality training for the R&D department.

7. **Contract Renewals:** Detail the process for renewing employment contracts.

8. **Crisis Management:** Offer steps for communication during unexpected company-wide emergencies.

9. **Cybersecurity Training:** Emphasize the importance of cybersecurity in a memo to all employees.

10. **Dispute Resolution:** Guide on the formal steps for dispute resolution between two staff members.

11. **Diversity Training:** Craft an agenda for a workshop focusing on fostering workplace diversity.

12. **Dress Code Changes:** Inform employees about the relaxed summer dress code.

13. **Employee Assistance Program:** Promote the resources available through the employee assistance program.

14. **Employee Grievance:** Detail the process for reporting and resolving an employee grievance.

15. **Employee Health Checks:** Schedule mandatory annual health checks for all staff members.

16. **Employee Recognition:** Suggest innovative ways to recognize and reward standout employees.

17. **Employee Referral Program:** Describe the benefits and guidelines of our employee referral program.

18. **Employee Resignation:** Provide a checklist to be followed when an employee resigns.

19. **Employee Sabbatical:** Detail the process and criteria for applying for a sabbatical.

20. **Employee Surveys:** Create questions for a survey on workplace satisfaction.

21. **Flexible Work Hours:** Promote the adoption of flexible work hours for improved work-life balance.

22. **Harassment Claims:** Lay out the procedure when an employee reports workplace harassment.

23. **Health and Wellness Day:** Propose a schedule for a day dedicated to employee health and wellness.

24. **Hiring Drive:** Detail strategies to attract top talent during our next hiring drive.

25. **Holiday Season:** Propose ways to maintain productivity during the holiday season.

26. **Inclusivity Workshops:** Plan a series of workshops on inclusivity and allyship in the workplace.

27. **Internal Job Postings:** Encourage employees to consider internal job postings for career growth.

28. **Layoffs:** Script a sensitive message for managers to address departmental layoffs.

29. **Maternity/Paternity Leave:** Describe our company's maternity/paternity leave policies.

30. **Mental Health Awareness:** Craft a message emphasizing the importance of mental health.

31. **Mergers & Acquisitions:** Discuss how to assure employees during company mergers.

32. **New Policy Introduction:** Inform employees about the introduction of a new workplace policy.

33. **Office Relocation:** Inform staff about the logistics and benefits of our office relocation.

34. **Onboarding Process:** Describe the process for onboarding a new employee in the IT department.

35. **Overtime Regulations:** Clarify regulations and compensation related to overtime.

36. **Performance Improvement Plan:** Describe steps for employees placed on a performance improvement plan.

37. **Promotions:** Define the criteria considered for promoting an employee to a managerial position.

38. **Religious Accommodations:** Address the accommodations available for various religious observances.

39. **Relocation:** Guide employees on the essentials when relocating to our overseas branch.

40. **Remote Work Transition:** Offer guidance on transitioning to a permanent remote work setup.

41. **Retirement Planning:** Outline a seminar on retirement planning for senior employees.

42. **Retrenchment:** Script a message addressing the difficult decision of company retrenchments.

43. **Safety Protocols:** Reinforce the importance of adhering to safety protocols in the factory.

44. **Salary Negotiation:** Offer tips for conducting a successful salary negotiation with potential hires.

45. **Team Building:** Suggest exercises for a team-building offsite for the marketing department.

46. **Team Conflict:** Advise on resolving a conflict that's arisen within a project team.

47. **Training Development:** Plan a curriculum for improving soft skills among employees.

48. **Union Negotiations:** Prepare for the upcoming negotiations with the employee union.

49. **Volunteer Opportunities:** Share upcoming volunteer opportunities for employees.

50. **Workshop Feedback:** Gather feedback on the recent communication skills workshop.

4.4 Task

What it is: Task specifies the action you want the persona to perform. It sets the direction and defines the objective of the interaction, whether it's generating content, providing information, or solving a problem.

Significance: Task clarifies your intent and ensures that the persona delivers the desired outcome. It prevents ambiguity in the interaction.

Role: The task element guides the persona in understanding the goal of the prompt, allowing it to generate responses that align with the intended action. For example, if the task is to summarize a document, the persona knows to condense the content.

List of Tasks

1. Advise	2. Allocate	3. Analyze
4. Assess	5. Calculate	6. Collate
7. Compare	8. Compile	9. Coordinate
10. Define	11. Describe	12. Design
13. Determine	14. Develop	15. Draft
16. Enhance	17. Establish	18. Evaluate
19. Explain	20. Facilitate	21. Finalize
22. Forecast	23. Formulate	24. Gather
25. Identify	26. Illustrate	27. Incorporate
28. Integrate	29. Interpret	30. List

31. Map	32. Measure	33. Monitor
34. Optimize	35. Organize	36. Plan
37. Prioritize	38. Propose	39. Recommend
40. Refine	41. Report	42. Research
43. Review	44. Schedule	45. Streamline
46. Structure	47. Summarize	48. Synthesize
49. Update	50. Visualize	

1. **Advise:** Advise on the legal considerations when terminating an employee.

2. **Allocate:** Allocate funds for various employee wellness programs.

3. **Analyze:** Analyze the feedback from the recent employee satisfaction survey.

4. **Assess:** Assess the need for additional staff during the holiday season.

5. **Calculate:** Calculate the turnover rate for the past quarter.

6. **Collate:** Collate the feedback from exit interviews conducted in the last six months.

7. **Compare:** Compare the benefits of in-house training vs. external workshops.

8. **Compile:** Compile a list of recommended readings for leadership development.

9. **Coordinate:** Coordinate logistics for the upcoming team-building retreat.

10. **Define:** Define the competencies required for a project manager role.

11. **Describe:** Describe the benefits of a flexible working schedule.

12. **Design:** Design a feedback form for an upcoming training session.

13. **Determine:** Determine the factors affecting employee morale during the recent project.

14. **Develop:** Develop an onboarding checklist for new hires.

15. **Draft:** Draft a job description for a Data Analyst role.

16. **Enhance:** Enhance the current employee referral program with better incentives.

17. **Establish:** Establish criteria for the Employee of the Month award.

18. **Evaluate:** Evaluate the pros and cons of remote work based on recent surveys.

19. **Explain:** Explain the company's policy on maternity and paternity leave.

20. **Facilitate:** Facilitate a focus group to discuss potential improvements in the workplace.

21. **Finalize:** Finalize the list of attendees for the HR technology webinar.

22. **Forecast:** Forecast the HR department's budget for the next fiscal year.

23. **Formulate:** Formulate a strategy for increasing representation of minority groups in leadership roles.

24. **Gather:** Gather testimonials from employees for the company's recruitment webpage.

25. **Identify:** Identify the gaps in our current diversity and inclusion initiatives.

26. **Illustrate:** Illustrate the company's growth in diversity hires over the past two years.

27. **Incorporate:** Incorporate feedback into the revised performance appraisal form.

28. **Integrate:** Integrate the new diversity and inclusion policies into the onboarding process.

29. **Interpret:** Interpret the data from the latest employee satisfaction survey to identify areas of concern.

30. **List:** List the steps involved in the recruitment process.

31. **Map:** Map out the career progression for a marketing associate.

32. **Measure:** Measure the impact of the new training module on sales performance.

33. **Monitor:** Monitor the feedback from remote workers regarding their challenges.

34. **Optimize:** Optimize the recruitment process to shorten the time-to-hire.

35. **Organize:** Organize the data from the recent compensation benchmarking survey.

36. **Plan:** Plan the agenda for the upcoming HR team offsite.

37. **Prioritize:** Prioritize the training needs based on feedback from department heads.

38. **Propose:** Propose a theme for the annual company retreat.

39. **Recommend:** Recommend ways to improve employee engagement.

40. **Refine:** Refine the criteria used for performance-based bonuses.

41. **Report:** Report on the yearly uptake of the company's learning and development budget.

42. **Research:** Research the latest trends in performance management.

43. **Review:** Review the feedback on our wellness program and suggest improvements.

44. **Schedule:** Schedule interviews for the shortlisted candidates for the sales team.

45. **Streamline:** Streamline the grievance redressal process to make it more efficient.

46. **Structure:** Structure a mentorship program for junior employees.

47. **Summarize:** Summarize the key points from the last team meeting.

48. **Synthesize:** Synthesize insights from various employee feedback platforms.

49. **Update:** Update the employee handbook to reflect recent changes in company policy.

50. **Visualize:** Visualize the company's growth in employee numbers over the past five years using a chart.

4.5 Output Format

What it is: Output format defines how you expect the persona to present its response, such as text, tabular content, comparison table, audio, visual, or structured data.

Significance: Output format ensures that the persona's response is compatible with your needs and intended use, making the interaction practical and valuable.

Role: The output format element instructs the persona on how to format its response for optimal usability. For instance, if you require a comparison table between two concepts, the persona will generate a suitable tabular output comparing the two concepts against a set of parameters for comparison.

List of output format

1. Agenda	2. Bullet Points	3. Case Study
4. Checklist	5. Comparison Table	6. Decision Tree Explanation
7. Dialogue Conversation	8. Evaluation Criteria	9. FAQ Format
10. Feedback Form Text	11. Flow Description	12. Glossary
13. Guidelines	14. Histogram Description	15. Job Posting
16. Letter	17. Matrix	18. Meeting Minutes
19. Multiple Choice Questions	20. Narrative	21. Numbered List

22. Organizational Chart Description	23. Policy Statement	24. Pro / Con List
25. Proposal	26. Quiz	28. Ranking
29. Recommendation	30. Reflection	31. Report Format
32. Review	33. Role Play Script	34. Scatter Plot Description
35. Scenario Description	36. Step-by-Step	37. Strategy Outline
38. Suggestion Box	39. Summary	40. Survey Questions
41. SWOT Analysis	42. Table	43. Testimonial
44. Timeline	45. Training Module Outline	46. Tree Map Description
47. True or False Questions		

1. **Agenda:** Create an agenda for a diversity training workshop.

2. **Bullet Points:** List the key responsibilities of an HR manager.

3. **Case Study:** Write a case study about a successful employee retention strategy.

4. **Checklist:** Create a checklist for an effective onboarding process.

5. **Comparison Table:** Compare full-time, part-time, and contract employment.

6. **Decision Tree Explanation:** Outline a decision tree for

handling employee disputes.

7. **Dialogue/Conversation:** Simulate a conversation between an employee and HR about a leave application.

8. **Evaluation Criteria**: List criteria for evaluating a training session's effectiveness.

9. **FAQ Format:** Draft a FAQ for the company's new performance appraisal system.

10. **Feedback Form Text:** Draft textual feedback prompts for an employee engagement activity.

11. **Flow Description:** Describe the flow of the recruitment process.

12. **Glossary:** Draft a glossary of common HR terminologies.

13. **Guidelines:** Write guidelines for effective team communication.

14. **Histogram Description:** Describe the age distribution of employees.

15. **Job Posting:** Create a job posting for a Benefits Coordinator.

16. **Letter:** Draft a letter addressing changes in the company's health benefits.

17. **Matrix:** Build a skills matrix for a project manager position.

18. **Meeting Minutes:** Simulate meeting minutes of an HR brainstorming session.

19. **Multiple Choice Questions:** Craft questions to assess employee understanding of workplace safety protocols.

20. **Narrative:** Describe a day in the life of an HR intern.

21. **Numbered List:** Create a numbered list of various types of leaves available in India.

22. **Organizational Chart Description:** Describe the hierarchical structure of the company.

23. **Policy Statement:** Craft a statement on the company's stance on diversity and inclusion.

24. **Pro/Con List:** Highlight the pros and cons of flexible working hours.

25. **Proposal:** Write a proposal for initiating a mentorship program.

26. **Quiz:** Draft a quiz to test knowledge about company policies.

27. **Ranking:** Rank the top 5 employee benefits in terms of popularity.

28. **Recommendation:** List recommendations for improving employee well-being.

29. **Reflection:** Write a reflection on the outcomes of the recent performance reviews.

30. **Report Format:** Draft a report on the latest employee engagement survey results.

31. **Review:** Write a review on a recent HR tech tool the company adopted.

32. **Role Play Script:** Write a script for a role play on effective negotiation.

33. **Scatter Plot Description:** Explain the correlation between

employee training hours and performance ratings.

34. **Scenario Description:** Describe a hypothetical scenario where a team resolves a conflict.

35. **Step-by-Step:** Explain step-by-step how to submit a medical insurance claim.

36. **Strategy Outline:** Draft an outline for the upcoming talent acquisition strategy.

37. **Suggestion Box:** Simulate suggestions from employees on improving the office environment.

38. **Summary:** Summarize the feedback from the last HR town hall.

39. **Survey Questions:** Design questions for an employee satisfaction survey.

40. **SWOT Analysis:** Analyze the SWOT of the current training and development strategy.

41. **Table**: Create a table of Pros and Cons of a Remote working policy.

42. **Testimonial:** Draft a testimonial from an employee who attended a leadership workshop.

43. **Timeline:** Describe a timeline of the company's diversity initiatives over the past 5 years.

44. **Training Module Outline:** Detail an outline for a training module on conflict resolution.

45. **Tree Map Description:** Explain the breakdown of the annual HR budget.

46. **True or False Questions:** Develop questions to quiz employees on code of conduct.

4.6 Tone of the Output

What it is: The tone of the output sets the mood and style of persona's response. It influences how the information is conveyed, whether it's formal, informal, persuasive, or informative.

Significance: Tone shapes the communication style, making it more relatable and appropriate for the intended audience or purpose.

Role: The tone element guides the persona in selecting the language, style, and expression to match the desired tone. For instance, a persuasive tone might be employed in marketing content, while an informative tone is suitable for educational materials.

List of the Tone of Output

1. Advisory	2. Analytical	3. Apologetic
4. Appreciative	5. Assertive	6. Authoritative
7. Casual	8. Cautious	9. Celebratory
10. Concise	11. Confident	12. Consoling
13. Critical	14. Curious	15. Detailed
16. Direct	17. Educational	18. Empathetic
19. Empowering	20. Encouraging	21. Enthusiastic
22. Explanatory	23. Firm	24. Formal
25. Friendly	26. Gentle	27. Grateful
28. Holistic	29. Humorous	30. Inquisitive

31. Inspirational	32. Introspective	33. Lighthearted
34. Motivational	35. Neutral	36. Nostalgic
37. Objective	38. Optimistic	39. Patient
40. Pensive	41. Persuasive	42. Professional
43. Reassuring	44. Relaxed	45. Respectful
46. Sarcastic	47. Skeptical	48. Supportive
49. Tactful	50. Urgent	

1. **Advisory:** Recommend ways for employees to maintain work-life balance.

2. **Analytical:** Break down the results of the last employee satisfaction survey.

3. **Apologetic:** Apologize for any confusion caused by recent policy updates.

4. **Appreciative:** Show gratitude to employees for their adaptability during remote work.

5. **Assertive:** State the mandatory nature of upcoming compliance training.

6. **Authoritative:** Lay down the company's stance on breach of confidentiality.

7. **Casual:** So, what's the deal with these new work-from-home guidelines?

8. **Cautious:** Advise on navigating office politics without stepping on toes.

9. **Celebratory:** Highlight the achievements of the team during

a successful project completion.

10. **Concise:** Summarize our company's diversity initiatives.

11. **Confident:** State the achievements of our HR department over the past year.

12. **Consoling:** Offer condolences and support after an employee's personal loss.

13. **Critical:** Evaluate the shortcomings in our current conflict resolution mechanisms.

14. **Curious:** Pose questions about how employees feel regarding the new office layout.

15. **Detailed:** Give me an in-depth explanation of our health benefits.

16. **Direct:** What are the steps for reporting harassment in the workplace?

17. **Educational:** Teach the basics of workplace ethics to new hires.

18. **Empathetic:** Help me understand the concerns of an employee facing personal issues.

19. **Empowering:** Empower staff by emphasizing their role in company success.

20. **Encouraging:** Boost morale after a tough quarter with a message of resilience.

21. **Enthusiastic:** Express excitement about our upcoming team-building retreat!

22. **Explanatory:** Clarify the reasons behind the recent shift in work hours.

23. **Firm:** Emphasize the zero-tolerance policy towards any form of discrimination.

24. **Formal:** Kindly elucidate the various stages in the employee appraisal process.

25. **Friendly:** Hey there! Can you walk me through our leave policies?

26. **Gentle:** Softly remind employees of the etiquette for communal spaces.

27. **Grateful:** Express thanks for the team's dedication during crunch periods.

28. **Holistic:** Provide a comprehensive view of career growth opportunities in the firm.

29. **Humorous:** Give me a light-hearted take on the challenges of HR management.

30. **Inquisitive:** Probe deeper into reasons behind low attendance at HR webinars.

31. **Inspirational:** Inspire with tales of employees who rose through the ranks.

32. **Introspective:** Delve into the importance of mental health awareness in the workplace.

33. **Lighthearted:** Offer a breezy take on the quirks of office culture.

34. **Motivational:** Inspire me with the importance of teamwork in our company.

35. **Neutral:** Present the facts about recent changes in our employment contracts.

36. **Nostalgic:** Reminisce about the company's milestones over the past decade.

37. **Objective:** State the pros and cons of biannual versus annual appraisals.

38. **Optimistic:** Share a hopeful perspective on post-pandemic workplace changes.

39. **Patient:** Reiterate the importance of completing mandatory training modules.

40. **Pensive:** Reflect on the impact of continuous learning in career development.

41. **Persuasive:** Convince an employee of the benefits of attending a workshop.

42. **Professional:** Please provide an overview of our company's recruitment process.

43. **Reassuring:** Comfort an employee anxious about job stability during company mergers.

44. **Relaxed:** Ease into an explanation of the extended holiday break.

45. **Respectful:** Address the concerns of older employees adjusting to new tech.

46. **Sarcastic:** "Another coffee machine broken? What a shocker!"

47. **Skeptical:** Question the effectiveness of open-office setups.

48. **Supportive:** Assure an employee of the company's support during tough personal times.

49. **Tactful:** Address recent layoffs while ensuring minimal panic among the remaining staff.

50. **Urgent:** Immediate steps to take if an employee tests positive for COVID-19.

ILLUSTRATIONS

Here given are some illustrations of crisp prompts created using some of the above elements, to achieve various corporate tasks:

1. **Sales Pitch Template:** Create a template for our sales team to craft compelling sales pitches.

2. **Sales Territory Mapping:** Design a tool to help our sales team visualize and optimize their territories.

3. **Sales Performance Dashboard:** Develop a dashboard to monitor and analyze sales team performance metrics.

4. **Customer Relationship Management (CRM) Integration:** Integrate our CRM system with our sales processes for seamless customer interactions.

5. **Marketing Campaign Planner:** Build a tool to plan and track the progress of marketing campaigns.

6. **Content Calendar Template:** Create a content calendar to organize and schedule marketing content.

7. **Market Research Survey:** Develop a survey to gather insights for market research and analysis.

8. **Social Media Analytics Dashboard:** Design a dashboard to monitor the effectiveness of our social media marketing efforts.

9. **Expense Report Form:** Create a standardized form for employees to submit expense reports.

10. **Financial Forecasting Model:** Develop a financial forecasting model to assist in budget planning.

11. **Vendor Evaluation Scorecard:** Design a scorecard to evaluate and select vendors for cost-effectiveness.

12. **Accounts Receivable Aging Report:** Generate a report to track outstanding customer payments.

13. **Inventory Management System:** Implement a system to optimize and manage our inventory levels.

14. **Shipment Tracking Tool:** Create a tool for customers to track the status of their shipments.

15. **Route Optimization Algorithm:** Develop an algorithm to optimize delivery routes for our drivers.

16. **Warehouse Safety Checklist:** Design a checklist to ensure safety protocols are followed in our warehouses.

17. **Customer Feedback Survey:** Develop a survey to gather feedback on customer service experiences.

18. **Service Level Agreement (SLA) Template:** Create a template for SLAs to set clear service expectations.

19. **Customer Support Knowledge Base:** Establish a knowledge base to empower customers with self-help resources.

20. **Service Request Management System:** Implement a system to streamline and track customer service requests.

21. **Attendance Tracker:** Design an attendance tracker that accommodates different shift schedules.

22. **Career Development Plan:** Create a structured career development plan for mid-level managers.

23. **Code of Conduct**: Create a comprehensive code of conduct emphasizing ethical behavior.

24. **Compensation Breakdown:** Create a compensation breakdown including both monetary and non-monetary benefits.

25. **Confidentiality Agreement:** Create a standard confidentiality agreement for employees in sensitive roles.

26. **Conflict Resolution Procedure:** Draft a standard procedure for resolving inter-departmental conflicts.

27. **Crisis Management Protocol:** Design a protocol detailing steps during company-wide emergencies.

28. **Cultural Sensitivity Training Module:** Design a module emphasizing cultural sensitivity for global teams.

29. **Diversity and Inclusion Report:** Design a format to present our annual diversity metrics.

30. **Employee Assistance Program Brochure:** Draft an informative brochure on our employee assistance offerings.

31. **Employee Event Proposal:** Create a proposal for an inter-departmental cultural exchange event.

32. **Employee Feedback Form:** Create a feedback form for employees to suggest workplace improvements.

33. **Employee Grievance Form:** Create a form for employees to confidentially report grievances.

34. **Employee Handbook:** Draft a comprehensive employee handbook detailing our company policies and values.

35. **Employee Offboarding Checklist:** Design a checklist to ensure smooth transition during employee offboarding.

36. **Employee Profile Template:** Create a template to maintain profiles of employees across global offices.

37. **Employee Recognition Certificate:** Design a certificate to recognize outstanding employee contributions.

38. **Employee Referral Program Guidelines:** Draft guidelines encouraging employees to refer potential hires.

39. **Employee Relocation Package:** Detail the benefits offered in our employee relocation package.

40. **Employee Survey Results:** Design a presentation showcasing the results of the annual employee satisfaction survey.

41. **Employee Transfer Request Form:** Draft a form for employees requesting inter-departmental transfers.

42. **Employee Wellness Initiative Outline:** Draft an outline of wellness initiatives planned for the quarter.

43. **Exit Interview Questionnaire:** Draft an exit interview questionnaire to gain insights from departing employees.

44. **Feedback Action Plan:** Design a plan to implement feedback received during the last town hall.

45. **Health and Safety Policy:** Design our company's health and safety policy to align with international standards.

46. **Internal Communication Memo:** Draft a memo template for department-wide communications.

47. **Internal Job Posting Announcement:** Draft an announcement for a managerial position opening in marketing.

48. **Job Description Template:** Draft a template for job descriptions applicable to various roles.

49. **Job Rotation Proposal:** Draft a proposal for implementing job rotation to boost cross-training.

50. **Learning and Development Calendar:** Design a yearly calendar of all internal training opportunities.

51. **Mentorship Program Outline:** Design a mentorship program to guide junior staff.

52. **Onboarding Checklist:** Create an onboarding checklist for new hires joining the finance department.

53. **Organizational Chart:** Design an organizational chart illustrating the company hierarchy.

54. **Performance Review Form:** Draft a performance review form emphasizing both skills and team dynamics.

55. **Probation Review Form:** Draft a review form for employees completing their probation period.

56. **Recruitment Strategy Plan:** Design a recruitment strategy plan to attract international talent.

57. **Remote Work Policy:** Draft a flexible remote work policy applicable to global branches.

58. **Retirement Plan Brochure:** Design a brochure explaining the benefits of our global retirement plan.

59. **Reward and Recognition Policy:** Draft a policy emphasizing our approach to employee rewards.

60. **Salary Benchmarking Report:** Design a report analyzing global salary benchmarks for our industry.

61. **Salary Increment Letter:** Draft a letter template announcing annual salary increments.

62. **Staff Meeting Minutes Template:** Create a template to record minutes during weekly staff meetings.

63. **Talent Development Plan:** Draft a talent development plan focusing on in-house training.

64. **Team Building Activity Schedule:** Draft a schedule for a month-long team building initiative.

65. **Team Charter:** Draft a team charter detailing values and goals for a new project team.

66. **Team Performance Dashboard:** Design a dashboard showcasing team performance metrics.

67. **Training Curriculum:** Design a training curriculum focused on leadership development.

68. **Training Feedback Form:** Create a feedback form for post-training evaluation.

69. **Vacation Leave Application:** Draft a vacation leave application form accommodating various leave types.

70. **Work-from-Home Guidelines:** Draft guidelines to ensure productivity while working from home

5 COMMON MISTAKES TO AVOID IN PROMPTING

Common Mistakes to Avoid in Prompting

The interaction between machine and man is just as important as the AI technology in the world of Artificial Intelligence. While we explored how to write great prompts in the previous chapters, it is also crucial to know what you shouldn't do.

In this section, we are going to explore the three major pitfalls that may block good communications with AI systems:

Vagueness: The Enemy of Precision	Over complication: Less is Often More	Context Ignorance: Knowing When and Where Matters

Vagueness: The Enemy of Precision

One of the biggest prompting errors is vagueness. An imprecise prompt will result in vague (or unrelated) answers from the AI and generate frustration and ineffectiveness.

Example

Vague Prompt: "Tell me something interesting."

AI Response: "The Earth orbits the Sun.

Although there is some "coolness" in AI's response it isn't helpful as the user expected it to be. A prompt more specific will make this response more concise.

Improved Prompt: "Can you tell me one cool thing about quantum physics?" (Note: In my experience talking to younger students, the word "cool" is a very effective way to engage their interest).

AI Response: "Quantum physics even states that particles can exist in multiple states at a time known as superposition." Did you know this?

If you're more specific, you are able to receive the information that you want.

Over complication: Less is Often More

The other trap is making your prompt more complex. Although it may feel like adding more information will give you a more precise answer, it can actually distract (or confuse) the AI.

Example

Overcomplicated Prompt: Give me a list of films which were released between 1990 to 2000, with action and comedy genres, and having a rotten tomatoes score over 80%?".

AI Response: "I'm sorry," the computer said, "I can't do that.".

Conditions within the prompt may be too many for the AI. It can be more effective to simplify it.

Simplified Prompt: "What are some '90s action or comedy movies with high ratings?

AI Response: "Okay, these are some of the highest rated action and comedy — 'Terminator 2', 'Dumb and Dumber', 'The Matrix', 'Toy Story' ".

Context Ignorance

Knowing When and Where matters. Failing to consider the context under which a prompt is generated can result in misunderstandings and incorrect responses.

Example

Context-Ignorant Prompt: "How's the weather?"

AI Response: "Where do you go?" I didn't know.

If your device has no information about your current location, the AI cannot give a relevant result. I think the prompt could've been more targeted and contextual.

Context-Aware Prompt: "What is the weather like in New York today?

AI Response: New York weather today's sunny and the temperature's a high of 75°F.

Add the context (e.g. location), and you'll get a better and more helpful answer.

Conclusion

Prompting effectively is an art that involves providing clarity, precision while maintaining context-awareness. By avoiding the pitfalls of being vague, overly complex and context-free, you are ensuring the best possible communication with AI systems to get the outcome you want. Keep in mind that the quality of the prompts you ask, will determine the quality of answers you get. So, craft your prompts wisely!

6

PROMPT FORMAT AND ILLUSTRATIONS

Prompt format

We have so far seen in detail those essential elements for composing a well-structured prompt to get the precise output. As clearly indicated in all the examples we have seen, well formatted prompts help you to communicate effectively with the AI tools.

In this section, let us see the art of composing well-crafted prompts by reviewing the essential elements that make them effective. Some practical illustrations demonstrating their real-world applications are provided by applying our learnings.

Let's get started!

Prompt Element Guidelines

- Clearly outline the persona your prompt suggests

- State your target audience clearly

- Establish the context

- Clearly describe the task

- State the desired output format, clearly

- Remember to mention the tone of the desired output

Based on the above format guidelines, a few illustrations are given below. Also showing how they are split into prompt element and content.

Illustration 1

Prompt for ChatGPT: Act like an **HR Consultant** and **analyze** the **employee turnover rates in the past year.** The response should be in a **bullet point list** format, written in a **formal and concise style,** targeted towards **Senior Management.** Keep in mind that the company has recently expanded into multiple international markets.

Prompt elements detailed:

Element	Content
Persona	HR Consultant
Audience	Senior Management
Context	The company has recently expanded into multiple international markets.
Task	Analyze the employee turnover rates in the past year
Output Format	Bullet point list
Output Tone	Formal and concise

Illustration 2

Prompt for ChatGPT: Act like an Employee Wellness Expert and recommend strategies to improve mental health at the workplace. The response should be a numbered list, written in an empathetic and encouraging style, targeted towards Department Leads. Remember, the organization transitioned to remote work due to the pandemic.

Breakup in Table Format:

Element	Content
Persona	Employee Wellness Expert
Audience	Department Leads
Context	The organization transitioned to remote work due to the pandemic
Task	Strategies to improve mental health at the workplace
Output Format	Numbered list
Output Tone	Empathetic and encouraging

Illustration 3

Prompt for ChatGPT: Act like a Diversity and Inclusion Advocate and explain the benefits of a diverse workplace. The response should be in an infographic description format, with an inspirational and informative tone, aimed at Hiring Teams. Consider that the company aims to be an industry leader in inclusive hiring.

Breakup in Table Format:

Element	Content
Persona	Diversity and Inclusion Advocate
Audience	Hiring Teams
Context	The company aims to be an industry leader in inclusive hiring
Task	Benefits of a diverse workplace
Output Format	Infographic description
Output Tone	Inspirational and informative

Illustration 4

Prompt for ChatGPT: Act like a Talent Acquisition Specialist and list the top sources for recruiting technical talent. The response should be in a table format, with a clear and actionable tone, designed for the Recruitment Team. Understand that the company is opening a new tech hub in Berlin.

Breakup in Table Format:

Element	Content
Persona	Talent Acquisition Specialist
Audience	Recruitment Team
Context	The company is opening a new tech hub in Berlin
Task	Top sources for recruiting technical talent
Output Format	Table
Output Tone	Clear and actionable

Illustration 5

Prompt for ChatGPT: Act like an Employee Engagement Expert and design a feedback survey for remote workers. The output should be in a step-by-step guide format, with a supportive and approachable tone, geared towards Team Managers. Account for the fact that the company will have a mix of in-office and remote work in the future.

Breakup in Table Format:

Element	Content
Persona	Employee Engagement Expert
Audience	Team Managers
Context	The company will have a mix of in-office and remote work in the future.
Task	Feedback survey for remote workers
Output Format	Step-by-step guide
Output Tone	Supportive and approachable

Illustration 6

Prompt for ChatGPT: Act like a Payroll Specialist and clarify the process of overtime pay calculation. The output should be in a Q&A format, written in a straightforward and informative style, intended for New Employees. Keep in mind that there are different overtime rules for part-time and full-time employees.

Breakup in Table Format:

Element	Content
Persona	Payroll specialist
Audience	New employees
Context	There are different overtime rules for part-time and full-time employees
Task	Process of overtime pay calculation
Output Format	Q&A
Output Tone	Straightforward and informative

Illustration 7

Prompt for ChatGPT: Act like a Corporate Trainer and draft a training module on effective communication. The response should be in a detailed outline format, with a motivational and interactive tone, meant for Mid-level Managers. Be aware that the company is focusing on cross-functional collaboration this year.

Breakup in Table Format:

Element	Content
Persona	Corporate trainer
Audience	Mid-level managers
Context	The company is focusing on cross-functional collaboration this year
Task	Training Module on effective communication
Output Format	Detailed outline
Output Tone	Motivational and interactive

Illustration 8

Prompt for ChatGPT: Act like a Benefits Coordinator and illustrate the differences between health insurance options available. The output should be in a comparison chart format, written in a neutral and thorough style, and intended for Full-Time Staff. Note that there have been recent changes to the national health regulations.

Breakup in Table Format:

Element	Content
Persona	Benefits Coordinator
Audience	Full-Time Staff
Context	There have been recent changes to the national health regulations
Task	Differences between health insurance options
Output Format	Comparison chart
Output Tone	Neutral and thorough

Illustration 9

Prompt for ChatGPT: Act like an HR Analytics Expert and predict future hiring trends based on current data. The response should be in a report summary format, written in a data-driven and insightful style, geared towards the Strategic Planning Committee. Remember that the industry is undergoing rapid technological advancements.

Breakup in Table Format:

Element	Content
Persona	HR Analytics Expert
Audience	Strategic Planning Committee
Context	The industry is undergoing rapid technological advancements
Task	Future hiring trends based on current data
Output Format	Report summary
Output Tone	Data-driven and insightful

Illustration 10

Prompt for ChatGPT: Act like an Organizational Development Specialist and suggest ways to enhance team collaboration in a remote setting. The output should be in a bullet point list format, with an encouraging and proactive tone, tailored for Team Leads. Keep in mind the challenges faced due to different time zones.

Breakup in Table Format:

Element	Content
Persona	Organizational Development Specialist
Audience	Team Leads
Context	Challenges are faced due to different time zones
Task	Ways to enhance team collaboration in a remote setting
Output Format	Bullet point list
Output Tone	Encouraging and proactive

7

PROMPTING POSSIBILITIES

Prompting Your Way To Success

In this section, let's understand the five areas where prompts are widely used to make a change by addressing the specific needs or goals pertaining to them.

Depending upon the area suitable to your expertise, you will also be creating the prompts and using them. Those five areas shortlisted here are,

Productivity Prompts

Nowadays productivity is more than a buzzword, it's a requirement. The prompts in this category are aimed to help you automate your actions, create new ideas, and improve productivity. These prompts are created with an aim to be practical and can easily become part of your everyday routine in helping you skill up or improve your approach to digesting vast quantities of information, etc., generally improving the productivity in the day to day life/work.

Writer's Prompts

For seasoned and newbie writers alike, writer's block or finding inspiration is a tough enemy. The purpose of these prompts is to take some of the load off you by offering multiple prompts that focus on story concepts, character arcs, etc. Whether you need help in writer's block or you're just looking for some new ideas for the next blog post, these prompts will be helpful tools to kickstart your creativity.

Social Media Prompts

Social Media is an ever-evolving landscape and can be over-whelming to navigate. These prompts guide you into making entertaining content, get followers, & know the intricacies of each platform. If you're a media professional or someone wanting to improve their online presence, these prompts give you practical insights to up your Social Media Game.

Marketing Prompts

Being at the cutting edge is critical in the present world where marketing is highly competitive. Those prompts in this category will give tips on new ways to create a brand, how to attract customers, and how to plan your campaigns. Whether you have something new to release or you want to improve what you're doing now, these prompts are choc-a-block with ideas to make them come true.

Entrepreneurship Prompts

Entrepreneurship is an adventure full of adversity and opportunity. These prompts will guide you with actionable ideas for every stage of the entrepreneurial process, from idea to solution. Whether you have a startup or want to grow a business, these cues would be helping you with the decision making.

Conclusion

Based on the practical ways you have learnt in this book to create the best prompts suitable to every situation in the business and with the understanding of these focus areas, start creating your area specific prompts. These prompts will help you to achieve your work/personal objectives through the different AI tools available in the market.

8 THE FUTURE OF PROMPTING

The Evolving Landscape of Prompt Crafting

In the AI community, crafting prompts has been the hot topic and is considered by some to be "the job of the future". Its sustainability, however, is not agreed upon.

One Harvard Business Review article1 predicts that future generations of AI systems will be more intuitive at reading natural language, and hence less reliance on carefully crafted prompts shall be required. AI language models such as GPT-4 are already proving capable of generating prompts, thereby reducing the need for manual prompt generation by humans.

The Shift Towards Problem Formulation

According to the same article, one of the longer-lasting skills in the landscape is knowing how to frame problems — identifying, examining, and breaking down problems. With prompt crafting techniques, you are optimizing the textual input whereas with problem formulation you are identifying the problem area, the scope, and the bounds. This capability is key to successful AI adoption, but frequently under-invested in.

Prompting related Jobs Truth

I found another article2 at TechXplore asking if prompt crafting is even an actual thing or worth getting into. But while the job market for people skilled in prompts hasn't blown up quite as much as some had predicted, people in such roles as machine-learning engineer or AI specialist have ended up working in creating prompts. The article argues that there are two kinds of contributors in the field of prompt engineering: domain experts who add value to the field, and technical experts who add value to the field.

The Importance of Adaptability

With AI models continuing to mature, the methods of prompting will need to change as well. If you're from an end-user domain or having a technical background, you should be aware of the current and emerging trends happening in the AI space since they help you in building better prompts.

The Rise of Context-Aware Systems

Now with the advancement of AI tools and systems, they are becoming smarter to understand context. The future could see the need for less direct prompting, and more native, conversational communications. For example, instead of asking a virtual assistant "What's the temperature in New-York today?" is replaced by "Do I need an umbrella in New-York, today?".

Ethical Considerations in Prompting

With AI integrated into the fabric of our daily lives, ethical questions around prompting will rise. This means avoid asking prompts that can generate negative or biased answers. Ethical cueing is likely to be a subspecialty, dealing with how to interact with AI tools ethically.

Industry-Specific Prompting

Further integration of AI in health care, finance and other legal services will see the emergence of trade-specific prompts. The prompt crafter's role will be even more specialized, because these prompts will need in-depth industry knowledge, including terms of art, compliance, and bespoke design considerations.

Role of Data in Prompting

Prompt effectiveness will be influenced more and more by data analytics. With advanced analytics we'll be able to figure out what the better prompts are and why, paving way for a science-based prompt design.

The Human-AI Collaboration in Prompting

It's not just about AI tool learning to understand humans even more, it's also about people learning to ask the right questions of AI tools. Schooling and seminars on how to ask in a manner most suited to a generative AI system will be widespread as people in the general population grow used to talking to AI tools.

The Globalization of Prompting

The demand to see prompts translated into other languages and culturally appropriate will increase as AI becomes more and more ubiquitous. In addition to the language, prompt crafters will have to think about local cultural context when they're designing prompts for a broad cross-cultural user base.

By understanding these trends and their implications, you can better prepare for the ever-changing AI landscape, ensuring that your skills and strategies are not only effective but also adaptable to the future of prompting.

References:

1.   https://hbr.org/2023/06/ai-prompt-engineering-isnt-the-future

2.   https://techxplore.com/news/2023-08-prompt-ai-job-future-short-lived.html

9 KEY TAKEAWAYS AND NEXT STEPS

Key Takeaways

As "The Prompting Playbook – Fueling Imagination through Generative AI" comes to an end, let us pause to contemplate on the journey that we've undertaken together. We've covered a lot of territory — from basic knowledge of what a prompt is, to deeper dives into structured prompting.

We've looked at different prompt types — open-ended, closed-ended, and command prompts — all with different benefits. We've also looked at the theory and practice of creating great prompts, with an emphasis on the need for clearness, precision, and context. We've looked at actual examples in practice, to take away learnings for our own efforts in promoting.

Mastering the craft of prompting is vital. The more AI is integrated into our lives in areas such as healthcare and finance through to marketing and customer services, the better we need to be able to communicate with them. It's more than getting it right, it's about asking the right question.

Next Steps for Mastering Prompting

Practice, Practice, Practice

Well, the age-old saying "practice makes perfect" is indeed applicable, particularly in the world of AI and prompts. As you use

AI more and more, you get better at making prompts that result in useful and accurate answers. Expect yourself to "make" things, don't shy away from experiments, prototypes and sometimes failure. A question is an opportunity to learn one-upping in the craft of prompting.

Stay Updated

As the world is changing rapidly when it comes to AI, we should make sure to always get updated with the newest buzz in the field and the latest research.

Keep following industrial leaders; subscribe to AI newsletters; take part in webinars and conferences. Keep in mind that the Prompting Playbook is the base of which you can always learn more.

With over twelve years of experience as an expert in public speaking and effective writing, I can state that communication is transforming. And now, thanks to AI, the risks are greater, but so are the rewards. So do yourself a favour — dive in; up your prompting AI skill!

Thanks for sticking with me on this informative trek. Here's to all your achievements in prompting for AI tools and the future!

APPENDIX

GLOSSARY

Glossary of Terms

AI (Artificial Intelligence): The simulation of human intelligence in machines programmed to think, learn, and make decisions.

Algorithm: A set of rules or procedures that an AI follows to perform a task.

Chatbot: A software application designed to simulate human conversation.

Chat History: The record of previous interactions with the AI, which can be used for context.

Closed-Ended Prompt: A prompt designed to elicit a specific, often yes-or-no, response from the AI.

Conditional Prompting: The practice of using conditional statements in prompts to guide the AI's responses based on certain conditions.

Context: The surrounding information or situation that helps the AI understand the prompt better.

Command Prompt: A prompt that instructs the AI to perform a specific action.

Data Analytics: The process of examining data sets to draw conclusions and insights.

Data Privacy: The practice of ensuring that personal data is securely stored and managed.

Data Set: A collection of data used to train or test an AI model.

Deep Learning: A subset of machine learning that mimics the neural networks of the human brain.

Ethical Prompting: The practice of crafting prompts that avoid eliciting harmful or biased responses from the AI.

Fine-Tuning: The process of making small adjustments to an AI model after initial training.

GPT (Generative Pre-trained Transformer): A type of AI model designed for natural language understanding and generation.

Heuristic: A problem-solving approach that uses practical methods for finding sufficient solutions.

Machine Learning: A type of AI that enables a system to learn from data.

Metadata: Data that describes other data, often used for sorting and organizing.

Natural Language Processing (NLP): A field of AI that focuses on the interaction between computers and human language.

Neural Network: A computational model inspired by the human brain, used in machine learning algorithms.

Open-Ended Prompt: A prompt designed to elicit a more expansive, creative response from the AI.

Persona: A character or role that an AI can assume to interact in a specific manner.

Prompt: A question or instruction given to an AI to elicit a specific response or action.

Prompt Engineer: A person specialized in crafting effective prompts for AI interaction.

Sentiment Analysis: The use of natural language processing to identify and categorize opinions expressed in text.

Syntax: The set of rules that dictate how prompts should be structured.

Training Data: The initial set of data used to teach an AI model.

Use Case: A specific situation where a product or service could potentially be used.

User Interface (UI): The space where interactions between humans and machines occur.

Vagueness: The quality of being unclear or not specific, often leading to ambiguous AI responses.

Workflow Automation: The use of technology to automate complex business processes and functions.

General Q & A

1. **What is a prompt?**

    A prompt is a question or instruction given to an AI to elicit a specific response or action.

2. **Why are prompts important?**

    Prompts guide the AI in generating the kind of response or action you desire.

3. **What is an open-ended prompt?**

    An open-ended prompt is designed to elicit a more expansive, creative response from the AI.

4. **How is a closed-ended prompt different from an open-ended prompt?**

    A closed-ended prompt is designed to elicit a specific, often yes-or-no, response, while an open-ended prompt allows for more creative answers.

5. **What is conditional prompting?**

    Conditional prompting involves using conditional statements in prompts to guide the AI's responses based on certain conditions.

6. **Can I use multiple prompts in a single interaction?**

    Yes, you can use multiple prompts to guide a more complex conversation with the AI.

7. **What is prompt engineering?**

    Prompt engineering is the practice of crafting effective

prompts for better AI interaction.

8.   How do I avoid vague prompts?

Be specific and clear in your wording to avoid ambiguity.

9.   What are the ethical considerations in prompting?

It's important to avoid crafting prompts that could lead the AI to generate harmful or biased responses.

10.   Can prompts be biased?

Yes, if the wording or structure of the prompt contains biases, the AI's response may also be biased.

11.   How do I test the effectiveness of a prompt?

You can test a prompt by evaluating the relevance and accuracy of the AI's response.

12.   What is a use case?

A use case is a specific situation where a product or service could potentially be used.

13.   Can I customize a prompt?

Yes, most AI models allow for prompt customization to better suit your specific needs.

14.   What is a command prompt?

A command prompt is a specific instruction given to the AI to perform a particular action.

15.   How do I handle errors in AI responses?

Errors can usually be corrected by refining the prompt or

providing additional context.

16. **What is a persona in AI?**

A persona is a character or role that an AI can assume to interact in a specific manner.

17. **Can I use prompts for data analysis?**

Yes, prompts can be crafted to guide the AI in performing data analysis tasks.

18. **What is the impact of context on prompting?**

Context helps the AI understand the prompt better, leading to more accurate responses.

19. **How do I stay updated on prompting techniques?**

Following industry publications and experts can help you stay updated on the latest techniques and trends.

20. **Is there a limit to the length of a prompt?**

Different AI models may have different limitations on prompt length.

21. **How do I know if my prompt is too complicated?**

If the AI's response is off-target or nonsensical, the prompt may be too complicated.

22. **Can I use prompts for automation?**

Yes, prompts can be used to guide automated tasks and workflows.

23. What is the role of syntax in prompting?

Syntax rules help in structuring the prompt for better understanding by the AI.

24. Can I use AI for sentiment analysis?

Yes, specific prompts can be used to guide the AI in performing sentiment analysis.

25. What is fine-tuning in AI?

Fine-tuning involves making small adjustments to an AI model to improve its performance.

26. Can I use AI for content generation?

Yes, prompts can be crafted for various content generation tasks.

27. What is a heuristic approach in AI?

A heuristic approach involves using practical methods for problem-solving.

28. How do I ensure data privacy when using AI?

Make sure to use AI models and platforms that comply with data privacy regulations.

Notes

About my book "One Page Communicator" #1 Amazon Best Seller

Interaction with other human beings forms the very foundation of society, and throughout the course of history, communication has been pivotal to our evolution. Among the various facets of human behavior that have undergone significant changes during this evolution, one aspect that stands out is communication itself.

In the realm of business, the key to transforming your dreams into success lies in effective communication. The ability to communicate effectively is an esteemed skill, particularly at middle management and senior executive levels.

This book centers around the paramount importance of effective communication within organizations, specifically focusing on the concept of 'One Page Communication' (OPC) and its core components: the audience, message, and purpose. Given the abundance of information across numerous channels and mediums, professionals must strive to deliver compelling communication that not only fits within a single page but also serves its intended purpose.

Through this book, my objective is to share my experience in creating concise and coherent communication for diverse scenarios across various industry verticals, thereby demonstrating their effectiveness in fulfilling their intended objectives.

I cordially invite you to embark on this journey, as we explore this new era of corporate communication together!

Available in both paperback and Kindle versions globally.